TAMPED,

BUT LOOSE ENOUGH

TO BREATHE

TAMPED,
BUT LOOSE ENOUGH
TO BREATHE

poems

MARK TODD

CONUN
DRUM
PRESS

AN IMPRINT OF BOWER HOUSE

DENVER

Design and Illustration by Margaret McCullough

Library of Congress Cataloging-in-Publication Data on File
ISBN 978-1-942280-61-3

10 9 8 7 6 5 4 3 2 1

The "Prologue" and "Epilogue" from "John Wesley Hardin" previously appeared in *Wire Song* (Conundrum Press, 2001).
"A Chorused Flock of Birds" and "Under Saddle" appeared in the anthology *Open Windows, 2005* (Ghost Road Press); versions of "Like Sleep, But Brittle," "Runaway," and "Mountain Roads" in the anthology *Open Range: Poetry of the Reimagined West* (Ghost Road Press, 2006); "Deer Season" and "A Hunter's Song" in the July and November 2006 issues, respectively, of *Mountain Gazette*; "Tongues, Teeth, Knuckles" in 2006 and both "Renovations" and "Fresh Powder" in 2008, respectively, of the *Gunnison Valley Journal*; "Timorous Trigonometries" in *Rogues&Scholars Literary Journal* (January, 2011), and "Cold War Lies" in *Rogues&Scholars Literary Journal* (April, 2011).

INTRODUCTION

Former Colorado Poet Laureate Dave Mason once told me poets too often rush to publish work, which is seldom as ready as they think.

A number of poems in the earlier iteration of this volume reinforced Dave's point for me: Since the first edition of *Tamped* came out, I've had the opportunity to "test" the success of my lines at hundreds of readings both home and abroad, and on-stage delivery revealed rough spots that remained invisible so long as the words remained on the page. But before live audiences, I discovered my tongue was the truest proving ground for my words.

What a delight to have the chance to refine those poems in this new version of *Tamped* for Bower House, the result of repeated impromptu variations to smooth out lines while eyeing my listeners. And changes in syntax, diction, and cadence reshaped the contents for a number of poems in the current volume.

I've also added several new poems that ran the same performance gauntlet until I liked what they said and how audiences responded.

At the same time, I've worked to preserve what readers and audiences told me they liked best about these poems. My wife Kym has always been my fiercest and most honest critic, and she used to tell me my delivery voice sounded the same, and hence monotonous, and I worked hard to change my literal voice when

I started reading my work regularly for the public. And my delivery began to influence my writing and stretched the sense of craft in an interesting way for me. In fact, one reader later told me the different sections of *Tamped* felt like reading poems by different poets, and it's true—I collected these differing personas into the discrete sections making up the book, which I've preserved in the current version.

In addition to purposeful experimentation with differing voices for various poems, this version of *Tamped* retains the original's experimentation with a wide range of open and closed forms. W.H. Auden once offered what I consider the finest definition of poetry: the best possible words in the best possible order. My fascination with prosody began twenty-plus years ago, due in large part to David Rothman, who encouraged me to dip into the deep waters of the best possible order which form implies. At its core, that journey into myriad permutations of formal verse resulted in *Tamped*. Even today, I still feel like a novitiate, but that's what so engaging about the process. It's the striving rather than the final product that keeps bringing me back.

Gratefully, I've enjoyed several generous-spirited mentors along the way: foremost is David Rothman, who has always supported my work through personal suggestions, public opportunities, and referrals from his "Rolodex" of formidable contacts. Dave Mason has also been an important mentor, forgiving as well as generous, and I value his friendship, his inspiration, and his own marvelous words. I would also like to thank Dana Gioia, who has always taken time to offer both guidance and encouragement. Finally, I want to thank my two publishers—Matt Davis of Ghost Road, who believed the first iteration of these words deserved a book; and of course,

Caleb Seeling, who has continuously supported all my poems through praise and deed, and who now has allowed me to breathe new life into the pages of this volume for Bower House.

—mdt
Doyleville, Colorado, 2018

poems

window worlds

to tell the truth

Garbonelli's corpse

John Wesley Hardin

tamped, but loose enough to breathe

severed dreams

window worlds

TONGUES, TEETH, KNUCKLES

Fastened sleet sashes panes
and window-worlds outside,
where horses confront worse.
All night, their manes gathered
slush, wind-dreaded to hold

ice like tongues suspended
in syllables tinkling
bitter chill. A raw-boned
gelding lifts one front hoof
to batter into snow

while his other feet clamp
legs in narrow shadow.
The herd waits, enduring
winter teeth zippered tight
to February cold.

Behind them, breezes strafe
magpies, pushed against trees,
gusts strong enough to count
striped knuckles on willow
phalanges, clench by clench.

LIKE SLEEP, BUT BRITTLE

Like sleep, but brittle,
a film that crackles
from each toss to turn
and then returns
to starch and wakefulness.

And still the moon stalks
across the floor, its snarl
a predation of light
ready to sink claw shafts
into sleeping wood.

My shallow breaths
pull at the hours, each a gate
of brass and hinged shadow
that will not open
before time's andante knocks.

But a cat purrs warmth
into my back, kneads the ridges
of my spine with soft throbs,
as I drift, almost unaware,
on the margins of a thin night.

FRESH POWDER

Her face, luminous
with first-snow albedo,
flexes to smile at work
she's penned, laser-etched,

eager on sheets that paper
my desk, but her lines
still smooth the socket
and cornice of expression.

Words settle, blanket
pages until only flat
December ground remains. Soon,
she'll gather her thoughts

to walk under the blue
eye of day, careless to its rhythms
or how glare sculpts
powder from fresh words.

BUFFALO WORDS

start on horizons that shimmer
into form, rumble inward
terrain, become a herd
of thundering verbs, shaggy-humped

nouns quick to trope
or rampage through our brains,
the hordes trampling
platitudes. Unruly, bellowing

words, champing with havoc,
senew taut, rangy, red
eyes daring us to look
away, but we don't,

can't so long as their steamed
snorts sear verse breaths.
Words—droves of them spilling
over vast, untrodden speech.

A CHORUSED FLIGHT OF BIRDS

Startled aloft by clatter from the ground
    they wheel and climb, globbed by an unseen force
        that crowds them in a warping, flexing ball.
This harmony of sight requires no sound
    to guide their flock-together churning course,
        to tell them when to glide and when to stall.

The multitude, connected wing to wing,
    once joined, now flies apart as the group aborts
        the flight, dispersing, single in their fall,
their fluttered voice no longer massed to sing
        for all.

SUBLIMINAL AVIARY

Rough, like plucked goose flesh,
stray patches stripe paint
to *barn, swallow*ing brushed
edges in *red. Winged* with *black,*

*burd*ened shadows unhinge
doors perched over feathering
rust, *red tail*ings that *hawk*
wares long discarded, caged

inside careless years. Their
mute shades *rob, in* dusk, the once
limned vestments of work, leave
only emptiness where rafters

sag into *great horns, owl*ish
in vigilance—vacant raptors ·
with plumage flocked in silk,
filtered through entropy and time.

RENOVATIONS

I know summer has come
when my walls stain with daubed-
on mud, beads that layer
moistened plugs with sturdy
pockets of droplet brick.

The swallows have returned.
Their restless task: to build
new houses over mine.

With their chirp-throated songs
and busy industry,
they fashion an ancient
architecture, using
my planed, sanded aspen,
soffits on angled eaves
to fabricate aerie
villages in mere hours.

We draw our battle lines
each dawn, they erecting
nests anew, which I thrash
to crumbling clay by dusk,
shards covering the deck.

Each fresh undaunted day
the ritual repeats,
for four relentless weeks
until, at last, one day
the horde disbands, perhaps
puzzled why instinctual
diligence cannot win.

They leave, their broken rims
like Anasazi ruins,
abruptly abandoned
edificial kivas.

But I know I haven't
won. The first new next year
summer day, a fresh tribe
will wend its winging way
to my walls with daubed-on
moistened plugs, their throaty
chirps determined to build
new houses over mine.

BOUNDARY WATERS

A moving skirmish line:
thatched by branch tapestries
that build a wicker work
of twig-tangle and mesh,
filling the gaped hollows
in the creek, bank to bank,
water-stopping all flow.

Some nights, they gnaw saplings
to patch shut liquid seep,
dappling mud paste on leaves
as their pond home widens
and spreads bank boundaries
to smear rough contoured ground
with flat roofs that ripple.

Each day I breach new berms,
patted by moistened mouths,
marveling at their skill.
No chances for a truce,
so each night, I must sit,
hold one reluctant breath,
draw a bead, finger squeeze.

TEMPEST FUGIT

A blue-skied day
begins, then clouds,
scatters partly
in sheeted gray

with scuds that build,
drumming on ground
with drops too cold
to taste. Storms, filled

with thumps of wind,
bully their way
to open plains,
where squalls begin

to swell, to flash
against a distant
curtaining screen
of day soon passed.

DEER SEASON

It's why I keep a loaded gun, driving
roads heavy with winter, and nights.
Trails, hoof-packed and dark, must have led

to the glow of light scattered
from headlamps aimed road-straight.
She-ran-I-swerved to meet

dead center—a green-stick snap
that splintered my grill
and then her gracile pitch,

four legs arcing over the hood
while the tired rub of my wheels
locked down, she

glancing the roof to land
in the mirror of my rear view,
tufts shattered in flurries of deer

hair sleet.
   The silence, sudden.
Not road kill, not yet, her haunch

flinching below the moon's thin slice,
so I dragged her over a pebbled skin
of road and tar to the borrow ditch,

wondering if a tire iron would push
through her hide of labored breaths,
but folding legs instead, first hers

then mine, to sit and wait,
watching lunar wax
paint deer and snow and blood.

UNDER SADDLE

—for Habit, 1992-2005

A conversation I love to feel
through reins that reach a bit of steel:
to think a thing and the thing is done,
where horse and rider ride as one,
to know the motion of bone and heart
as muscled poetry and art.

Closing hands that finger leather
I hold his mouth as we move together.
He rounds his back to drive ahead
to stretch his trot, his legs aspread.
A fluent molten flowing horse
expressing me through equine force.

Seat-bone deep I sense the beat
of leading leg to cantering feet
as we shift in our stride to a tripling gait
as we stab with our hooves at the sand and the slate.
Collecting in our shared embrace
we ease into a slower pace.

For just a moment, in his hide,
the upward slope to every stride,
no difference now of me from beast,
I am the hoof and haunch released
to share our shared and common space—
renewed, regained, resolved, replaced.

FOUR ELEMENTS

it might have looked
this way a hundred times
a million years ago, contoured
land topped with red
brimmed liquid stone, at length
replaced by ancient seas
left to sink or drain away time

to the hollow Now that floats
with smoke, with a paste
of soot to smear ground far
from flame, no molten rims
to clench a four-year coming
drought, to paint summer
in palette hues of dun and hell

to tell the truth

BURGERBOY

maybe I would've pissed
myself if I'd've had time
to think about it more
than a second or two,
not that I hadn't come close
now and then, to standing
face to face with Burgerboy,
the name Kym gave
to Woody's big Black Angus bull,
though not the name our neighbors
would have called him,
if they called him anything,
and we knew it was our job
to fence him out.
but who'd've thought it?
a bull that size—
on the heavy side
of a ton, and more
it seemed, when you got up,
say, face to face now
and then, yeah more,
a lot more, and why
maybe I would've pissed
myself if I'd've had time.

not that I wasn't used
to seeing him standing there
looking on, and curious
like bovines tend to be.

even that first time
when we started to build
the place, and hadn't thought
of fences, just trying
to cut a line of sight
through the willows
for a telephone,
me holding down
a green and limber limb
while my buddy, saw
happy with his new
36-inch chain and hot
to see just how big
a swath he could cut,
him bearing down with a buzz
that shook me and the tree
'til, jeezus! we both looked up
to see that big black head
filling the hollow gap
between us and the swath
we'd cut, and which was all
it took to swing my buddy
and my buddy's saw
buzzing full around
to where my head was
only seconds before,
but I had fallen back
with the sudden sight
of Burgerboy, who didn't

seem to mind the noise,
just standing there,
big and black and curious,
and making me think
about what a good idea
fences were—yeah,
that was the first
but not the last
I would see of Burgerboy,
and not the time
I nearly pissed myself.

no, that time came
one mile of fence or two
and three summers later,
when the almost daily
routine was chasing Burgerboy
back to his side
of the pasture. those days,
and that was most days,
he just hopped
all two-thousand pounds
over my four- and in some
spots five-foot fence,
like he was jumping
a puddle. what a sight
to behold. like the time
Kym and I went
to the local rodeo and sat

straddling the eye-level
boards near the rough
stock gates, and one
bull unloaded his rider, then
ran-leaped-scrambled
over our fence not
twenty feet away. boy,
you couldn't see
the bull but you could
sure see the steady spew
of people in a climbing
hurry to the side without the bull.

so when Burgerboy showed up
one day, pushing his head
through the willows,
it was time for me and the dogs
to chase him out.
he knew the drill.
the dogs at his heels
and me with a piece
of handy branch to wave
in his direction, we headed
through a tunnel of trail
under thick-growth willows.
but then I took
a wrong-tunnel turn
and was the first to reach
the woven-wire fence, blocking

my own way—and that
was my first mistake.

so there I was, standing
in a narrow tunnel of trail,
before the mesh of fence,
in time behind me to hear.
the dogs yabbering
at Burgerboy's heels
and those heels in full
motion, thrashing down
the trail one instant,
just a rush of sound
stamping at broken branches
or snapping shoulder
high limbs to hollow
that tunnel even more,
and then the next instant
there he was in full view
and full charge
and heading my way.
me just standing
there, with an open jaw
full of mountain air,
which was my second mistake.

not that he had a mean
bone in his body, but I mean
those dogs had him

in so much of a lumbering hurry
that it was just easier
to overlook my trembling
body than the pestering yap
of those dogs—it didn't
look good, no, and then,
just then, was when
I would've pissed
myself for sure,
if I'd've had the time, that is,
but no, before I could
say "ohmygodamitey,"
I'm crunched down,
I'm cowering at the wire
and waiting for Burgerboy
to mash or strain
me through the mesh.
but his big black
one-ton Burgerboy body
cleared me and the fence
and then some, just
with a rocking horse
hop to land on the other side,
easy as you please, him
trotting on down the trail
with a tail-wring nonchalance.

—that's the time I almost pissed myself.

RUNAWAY

well I'd unhooked the trailer
just like I'd done a hundred times
I chocked the wheels
I set the block and cranked
it off the hitch
              so maybe it
did wobble just a bit, but still
just like I'd done
a hundred times before
I drove off down the slope

that's when my wife dropped
her pitchfork and ran
right past the truck
waving hands in the air
while the trailer aimed at two yearlings
watching from the fence's other side

there she was, just a little thing
but running to meet that thousand pounds
of trailer speeding down the hill
like her hundred pounds
and swinging hands could stop
its downhill speed
like it would take one look at her
and say, huh, and come to a halt

all the while, I looked on
and the yearlings looked on
watching her meet
the trailer meeting her
and all of us wondering
what would happen next

before I knew, I was backing
fast our one-ton truck
to block the trailer's roll

just in case my wife's hands failed

and trying to decide if those yearlings
would move before the trailer hit
the fence
            and how much would it cost
to fix the truck when a thousand pounds
of steel smacked hard into the bed

still rolling in reverse
my wife jumping to the side
yearlings not moving a step
the truck still in reverse

and then the trailer lurched
against the narrow rut
of borrow ditch and smacked
my hitch against the fender skirt
just as the trailer's wheels
bounced quick, ripped a tire
wide open as everything stopped
on top of the road

those yearlings standing
looking at the trailer
just in front of them

wife-truck-yearlings all okay

with just a fender dent
and ruined tire to show
how fast my heart was beating

SACRED RIDE

from the start we knew
it was an event to remember
and how many can say they lost
a whole tribe of indians
in just a couple hours?

but it didn't start
that way, no, it took
us a couple months
to get us ready to lose them
all, and all at once.

first, we had to ready
the horses, for it was horses
that the dream had been
about. not ours—theirs,
the indians, dreamt
inside wicker and cloth
by a holy man to make
the ride from holy place
to place, a trek on the backs
of cross-country mounts

so here we were, invited
to come along, but first
we had to condition
horses unaccustomed
(not that we were)
for a hundred miles
of country crossing
trails, and little of that
was marked on roads
that matched a map.

at last, all saddled down
with kids and dogs
and camping gear, we left
and drove our caravan
(a truck a car a trailer
stocked with stock)
across the parts of states
that separated us
from south dakota, driving
up on the appointed day
the day the ride was to begin

but didn't.

not then, not the appointed day
while we cooled our heels
camping near an elder
Elder friend we knew

so now just three days
of riding rough to make
the powwow a hundred miles
away, and one day gone
so thirty-three miles a day
but our elder Elder friend
told us, quit
acting like white guys,
which was hard
with Kym's blue eyes
and two toe-headed
kids in tow.

finally, adjusted to indian
time we saw the tribe
arrive but without enough
horse flesh for the ride so we spent
that day, the day we should have
ridden the first of thirty-three
miles, rounding up pasture ponies
who'd never seen a saddle
on their backs, no
problem, they said
we'll break them
as we go, and now the ride
was only two days before
the powwow and fifty miles
a day, yeah that would break
those pasture ponies in right.

we were up at dawn
and just bitting up
our nags when the rag
tag of the band came
thundering past and reined
in to see if they should wait
but I shouted, keep going
and we'll catch
up soon enough, and after
we cinch our mounts
so the leader shrugged and maybe
felt relieved not to try to stop
that pasture pony between his legs
who didn't seem sure
what stop meant anyway.

we couldn't have been ten
okay, maybe it was fifteen,
minutes before we headed
down the road with dust
still hanging over unshod
pony prints that tore
into the ground, man,
they were in a hurry
to get to that powwow now
so we broke into a feisty
trot and when we topped
the first hill they were already
over the second, at least

we had the roaded pony
prints to tell us they were up
there somewhere breaking
in those pasture ponies right.

so after five or six hills
we finally came to the end
of the road and the end
of any tracks or pony
prints just where the ground
turned into the broad
and south dakota rolling plains.
and we knew somewhere
out there to the east
was a cross-country band
of cross pasture ponies
hell-bent on a sacred ride
but way too far ahead
to pick a compass point
to know where fifty miles
would pitch their camp.

it was a mighty pretty
view, those rolling hills
and the farasyoucouldsee expanse
of south dakota, but the end
of our part of the sacred ride, because
we never saw those indians again.

THE DAY THAT DOG TOOK OFF

to tell the truth,
he didn't much care for dogs,
not little shit dogs,
and sneaky,
the way this one hid
and waited to pounce
from the bushes.
more like a cat.
but why have a dog
if it acts like a cat?
just get a dog,
which is what
he would have done

if his wife had asked him,
which she didn't,
the day she brought home that dog,
that little shit dog
that acted like a cat.

not that he didn't like cats,
or most dogs either, for that matter
– except maybe the one
his mama had brought him
home when he was only four,
the backyard full of dog
and always in his face,
licking him in the face full
until it grew up.

and then he was six,
with a full-grown dog
still full of the backyard,
knocking him down
as he screamed
in his ragged little-boy voice,
get it off! get it off!
until finally his mama came.

no, he didn't much care
for that dog, or this one either,

the day it took off,
the day he took it
for a walk, unleashed
and waiting in the bushes
along the trail,
along the willows by the creek.

But just when he was ready
for the pounce, he heard instead a yip!
and then again, yip!
a little further out and higher up
near the willow tops.
and that's when he saw,
along the creek, he saw
that little shit dog,
its legs scrambling
like a little toy

dog with its spring
wound too tight,
and with its thick coat
of little shit dog fur
all fastened to the talons
of an eagle's squeeze.

he watched the eagle stroke
its wings, hard
against the cool air
above the creek,
he watched
the bird-dog thing
dip a bit and disappear
behind the willow tops,
and then the sound
of water scratching pebbles
on the banks, drowning
out the yips that left him
in wonder at the sight—
that, and how ever
would he explain to his wife
what had happened
to her little shit dog.

THE COYOTE WHO WANTED TO BE A DOG

so it happened this way,
the coyote who wanted
to be a dog, back when
we lived below Coyote Hill,
which doesn't look like much
more than a bump
crow-flying from highway to hill,
but plenty still a hill
if you're steep-climbing on foot,
one hand-grasp of sage to the next
on the way to the top.

a west-flanking row
of lower tag-along ridges
nurses at Coyote Hill—
the ones Kym called
Coyote Pups,
and it happened then,
it happened when
we lived below the Hill
beside The Pups.

that summer we rode
every day—two riders
two horses two dogs—
along the backside mile,
no more, of The Pups
and dusty hot that year,
but out of the way

across a stretch that bordered
our neighbor to public land.

that's when we first saw
the coyote who wanted to be a dog.

it couldn't

have been much over a year old
and watching us at first
from rocks that creeped
the length and just below the ridge top.
we were two, three rides that way
and soon we saw it trotting
only half so far away
the length we rode along
The Pups, chattering and teasing
the dogs, who'd tear off
giving chase and meaning
business, and all the while
we'd shout at them,
get back, get back here!
but didn't do much good
once they had the scent.

and all of a sudden
that coyote pup turned, chased
the dogs, so surprised and tail-tucked,
part way back to us,

and quick—almost like a wheeling
flock of birds, flapping
against an empty sky
then changing course
on cue and all at once,
—that's how it looked,
that quick again,
but now against a canine sky of rock and sage,
the scene of dogs
who turn-tail chased or turn-tail fled,
a game of tag with rules
that only dogs and wannabes
could know. a game again
and again along the mile, no more,
that ran along The Pups.

everyday the same,
everyday the game—
two riders two dogs, no,
three, it seemed.
and soon enough
that pup became a trot-along
beside the dogs, a kind
of country escort for the mile
that flanked The Pups.

so we didn't think
about it much, just
the marvel of our traipsing troop,

until the day that yearling pup
didn't show
one day or the next,
didn't show
for all one week.

didn't show

until the dogs caught it,
the scent of it, I mean,
the carcass, I mean,
after it let our neighbor close enough
to put a bullet through its skull,

the coyote pup who wanted
to be a dog.

SOME FOLKS I KNOW

don't ask me if i know
these folks, i do, and parts
of them i just don't want
to know
       like looking at your hand
and knowing it's a helping hand
that does the things it should
without you asking for help

just jumps in and makes
the doing done without a word
and if need be the other hand
comes up quick and plays
its part since there's no end
to what you can do
with two hands working

but if you idle down
a bit and start to stare
at that hand there's things
you'd just as soon
not see
       that knobby thumb,
for one, or that twisted knuckle
that never seemed to straighten
out
   if only you'd give
it a rest it'd be fine

but no there you are
at the supper table
and you'd like
to ask for the bowl
of mashed potatoes
but then you'd have
to reach out that hand
and that's not the sort
of conversation piece
that seems to suit the food

all the same you know
you'll ask that hand
or maybe you won't
have to
        it'll just know
you need the help
next time you've got
something heavy to lift

well that's some folks
i know
        but don't ask
me, just find out yourself

Garbonelli's corpse

PART ONE — GABONELLI'S CORPSE

they didn't find the corpse
not right away
not right that day
and not that anybody gave
a tinker's dam
that he was dead
so when the aftermath
of lynching him had caked
with winter's snow

the work went on

they chiseled at the canyon wall
hard men breaking bones
on hard rock to notch
an angled trail
the narrow gauge could crawl along
could inch along
the shadows of the gorge
to reach the light
of flatter ground

and on the way they'd lost
by God
a dozen men more honestly

but still they'd looked away
beside the bridge
those men who traveled

from the camp-side to the town
and giddied-up the wagon
horses' pace
so no one had to see
the dangled rope and cut
like the spindle
of a weathered teat
no longer used
but stretched from use

though no one claimed
to be the one
who'd cut the weight away
or what they'd done
with what was left
of Garbonelli's corpse

hard men
breaking rock
or breaking bone
against the rock
while winter pushed
its paws through crusted snow
and sank into the mud of spring

by May the sky was blue
as columbines and still
no sign of Garbonelli's corpse

and then one Saturday
sun hitting the western-sided row
of Main Street stores
a row of wood-flat faces
squared like dominoes
and end to end
to hide the tented slant
of pitches from the street

that's when the smell
like an unseen ribbon
frayed and drifting
on the wind
drew flies then birds
and finally the men
who found the snow-
burned black
of Garbonelli's corpse
stashed there and propped
atop the mercantile
behind its store-front face
eyelids bloated shut
lips in a puckered pinch

like he could break
at any time
into a whistled song
without a care
that fine spring day

PART TWO — THE GAUGE OF MEN

it was Sawyer
who pushed
the men like he pushed
himself
     relentlessly
one more tie
one more spike
to brick the narrow grade
with wood and iron
to lay the tracks
like twinned metal tubes
their rigid side-by-side stretch
to sweep along
above the river run
and like the water below
to course with freight
and people's frothy dreams

but not until the road was done

he muscled his will
into the crew
bending their strength
into his own
to chip at the canyon walls
to make its bellied width
give way to men
hard men he could push
with a heavy hand

men who worked fought worked
and worked again

predawn tents retched out
their shadowed figures
as he'd count them out
and watched for those
he counted on

he liked the men
who worked without a word
their sinews bound to bone
there were others
men who paced the day
to give their tongues a chance
to sour all they said
and men of Garbonelli's sort
whose temper chased him
like a pack of dogs
with hollowed belly eyes
and quick to snap
at any scrap
of discontent

but Sawyer handled each
and each had wills
that fed the fire
that tie by tie
rail by rail

gave cadence
to the work
he channeled what he could
of smoldered words
and angry sparks
to work
to build
this thing
this road
its life now much his own

the gauge of men became his art
the building of this steam
which fueled the work
the building of the road
and payday
like the whistle of a train
would ease the steam
would let them coast
until he capped their fire again

they lined up for the dole
that was their pay
a crowd that narrowed
to a point
before the crate that served
to lay down coins
and give account

Sawyer kept his gaze
and steady
on the man ahead
as Garbonelli's cap
floating half a head
above the crowd
approached and pushed up front

and all the crew had known
the man wouldn't
not one whit
like the short-change he would get
but the man had slacked
and he would serve
example to the rest
and like it or not
there'd more than like
be trouble as that cap stood
daring and square
before the crate

no backing down now
for what would come

and then it came

PART III — FIST AND COIN

I only want
what's mine
he'd said
and fair
this railroad owes me
more than sweat
more than flesh
my body's drained
into the laying
of the track

I want the promise back
he'd said
a life for me and *cara mia*
that bastard foreman
he'd clench
if he could find
my very soul
he'd take the pennies
from my eyes
to build his road

he doesn't know
the life I build
by fist and coin
for *cara mia*
by fist to stand apart
to make them
stand aside

to give respect
how else to tilt
my chin up high
by coin to count
the days until
she joins me here
to lie with me again
and once again
to make a home
her hand in mine
my chin up high
we'll build a life
the two of us
on new-landed promises

that bastard thinks
he'll cheat me
from our plan but
by God
by fist
by coin
I'll bring her
to this land
I'll build a life
that we can share

we'll know respect
by fist
I'll see to that

we'll know a life
by coin
I'll see to that

PART IV — THE STORM

Mckee could hear
the ruckus up ahead
and shouting near the crate
palavering and words
that ranted crowded back
the men who circled
round the box
their voices rasping room
that hollowed out
a space for waving arms

Garbonelli's hands were full
of words and made
of gestures what his tongue
could hardly say

Mckee had never liked
the man apart
and scowling at the world
always quick to take
but never give
and here before the crate
before the foreman's book
he stood mad as hell
and twice as hot
there'd be no settling account
McKee and all the others knew
for Garbonelli's threats
had turned to shoves

and just the sort of thing
that breached the wall
between the master and the man

it was then
when Sawyer shoved him back
a boom slapped the foreman's chest
left him silent
wrapped him curled
in arms of smoke
sagged and settled
to his knees
but the eyes no longer saw

men rushed and tugged
the pistol from the grasp
of Garbonelli's hand
they all could feel the building storm
in the men's blood
in Mckee's blood
like a sudden mountain squall
like a storm that spills
unaware and unforeseen
across a ridge to wipe
the land with dark
with rage

a voice
(was it McKee's?)
had burst the pent-up flood
of pent-up shouts

the marching to the bridge,
the hands (McKee's?) that tied
and tossed the rope
that gave the shove
the taut and pluck
of weight made dead

as the rope hum-sawed
into the beam
but held against the sway
of Garbonelli's corpse

PART V — A LIQUORED JOKE

the spring is mild
is damp
is dampened more
by what the others found
atop the mercantile

I watch them try to wash
the winter memory away
with drink and poured
strong and raw into their throats

how like the man
they say
to find a way
to salt-rub wounds
for those who can't
just let it be
how like the man
they say
to rough the scabs
of healing guilt

but I sit quietly
the company of rye
enough
alone
and raise a silent toast
to Garbonelli's corpse

and not that we were friends
I'd only heard him speak
that once
that time
when I had bunked
with him
that time I took the pay
to them
but still it seemed
the thing to do

the meanness of it all

a liquored joke
I tell myself
to cut him free
to stash the corpse
up on the roof

the railroad crew
will soon be done
will soon be gone
they'll pitch their tents
out farther west

a liquored joke
perhaps
but sobering

a coward's way
perhaps
to humble them

to push them
on their way
to leave the town
to those who hope
to make a life
more permanent

my eyes seek out
first one
and then another
of the railroad crew
I stand I tip
my hat to strangers here
to men I know
by passing name
McKee and all the rest
all faces I have come
to know but soon
I can forget

once out the door
I walk the sidewalk boards
that hug the stores
I feel the way they hold
yet yield to stepping weight

tomorrow I will pay
respects to Garbonelli's grave

tonight I listen to the hush
that settles on the town
I listen to the cries
the nighthawks make
just past the borders of the town
in pastures and in meadows
the promise of the land
a land made home
for all who stay behind

John Wesley Hardin

PROLOGUE

"It was, of course, a wilder world back then,"
she said, and leaned back in her chair.
A hundred years, and more, of family tales
now separated early times from mine,
an era's end and when my mother's mother
knew his face, her older cousin Wes,
who bore the name of John, and Wesley Hardin.
But she was just a child when family said
he was the meanest man she'd ever know,
a Texas desperado, who'd won reprieve
though killing scores of men. Loyal to kin,
but homicidal still by all accounts.
Still, storied deeds had never told it all,
and she confessed that some accounts might add
a different view, the tales that left the man
and legended life unreconciled at best,
those stories partly told that made a cipher
of the man, the tales that we would never know.

MAGE

They's some that say black folk got no souls.
They say, we no better than dogs they keep
to lick their scraps when we not licking wounds.

But they wrong, they don't know the secret
I be telling you.
            You listen to me
cause I know, I know and don't you pretend
you cain't see me standing here beside you.
You listen good.
            They be a god—you hear?—
though She be black and dark as that new moon,
not spoiled by some splash of curded cream.

But She don't see me yet, not no ways
unlessen I find a way to wipe clean
off the white of that boy, to wipe the mean
of his white from my hands so's then my soul
be black again.
            How'd I come to know
we got souls? Maybe I tells you the secret.
Yes, I will, I will tell you the secret I knows.

That day be powerful hot—you listening?—

like the clouds be some big blanket and throwed
over a fire so's it trap all sort
of living thing. But long about evening
we start to stir and Uncle—well, he white,
but we all call him Uncle—so he say,

"Let's us have a wrastle match."

                      And we all say
"Yeah, yeah, let's wrastle."

                          But since it ain't fair,
me being a growed man and all, to stand
agin me alone, Uncle he then say,

"Wes, you and your cousin there, you both try
to pin Mage."

                   Wes, he saying how he can
do it hisself, but Uncle he make them
two boys, all scrawny and full up with spit,
tackle me.

               They wern't nothing, them two,
clambering all over me and I just
toss one aside like a potato sack,
and pin th'other, then pin 'em both, I does,
Wes squealing like a pig 'bout to be cut.
He be so red faced that he jump me again,
and I hold him down, whispering low like
in his ear so's Uncle don't hear,

                         "Your ass

too creamy white to pin Mage," I tell Wes,
which make him squirm hard, squirm like a bug
mashed with your thumb when you pull off its wings,
him yelling,

       "Get off! Get off!" And I does,
but slow like, and he jump-up-smack-me-hard
in the head, getting in his lick all smug
and righteous, his daddy being a preacher
and all.

       But I know that that ain't fair—no
not since the Construck-shun, not since the War
Between the Whites. His lick don't hurt me none,
but I begin to feel this weight a growing,
pressing me hard, like a strap pulled too tight
and hugging my chest—it be the sight of Wes
has done it, and I knocks him to the ground,
just one blow.

       "Mage!" Uncle he shout, but I says,

"I be free and what he done ain't right no more!
Nobody hit Mage since the Constuck-shun."

His cousins be holding Wes back, that boy
a swearing and a cussing and a swinging,
his fists flapping at the air.

       "Go home, Mage,"

Uncle he tell me. "You shouldna hit Wes.
And don't be causing grief, you hear me, boy?"

I mumble some, how it be Wesses fault,
and hangdog like, how I shouldna have to go,
leaving the festivities early on.
Then I look down and sees where Wes has tored
my shirt and I shout,
                    "Wes, he owe me
a shirt. See how it tored?"
                              "You go on, Mage,"
Uncle he say again.
                    So's I start
walking, kicking at rocks and such, looking
all sorrowful,
                    but long about sundown
and just as I be reaching this here bridge
I hear—clop, clop—a rider coming up.
I turn in time to see Wes bearing down
on me, riding that mount of his daddy's.
More horse than he have a right to saddle!
I quick jumps to the side and grabs them reins.

"Leggo, leggo, you black son of a bitch!"

Whoowee, that boy be riled up good,
but I see then, plain as the setting sun,
he be tracking me, so I says,
                              "Un-uh,

not til you pay me for the shirt you tored."
It be the one here. You sees the tored part?

"I ain't here to talk of shirts. I come
to teach you a lesson. Leggo my reins,
goddammit!"
                    But I hold on tight, smiling
big so's he know he ain't going nowhere.

Just then, he whip a pistol from his belt.
I don't hear no sound, just see the flash
of powder blazing out to cover me up,
to cover those eyes of his, and all twinkling
like two white stars, them eyes behind that grin.

I lay there purt-near most the night, I guess,
but then I get up, set here by the bridge,
stealing a look-see now and then at the heap
of my body laying there in the road.

I just keeps saying,
                    "Poor old poor old Mage.
Look what that boy is gone and done to you."

Uncle, him and his kin they come and take

me away, but you see I still be here,
setting by this here bridge.

                         And so I waits,
washing and a washing, trying to get
the white of wrastling Wes offen my hands,
so God know I be black. So's She take Mage
home.

                You hear me? You hear what I know?
Only, how does I wash off this white?

SHOOTERY

To pass the time one summer day
He walked to the street and called aloud
To gather round about the wall
And said he'd entertain the crowd.

He nailed the three of spades in place
And paced away with a whistled song.
He spun around, then quick as a blink
He fired three shots, three spades were gone.

He did the same to hearts and clubs
Then signed the cards and passed them out.
His shootery was clean and quick,
His expertise left little doubt.

Delighted children loved the trick,
The message chinked upon the wall.
But adults knew just what it meant
And none dared bother him at all.

MEASURE FOR MEASURE

Young Wes became a man too late
To fight for the Southern cause,
But when the War had ended, hate
Was strong for Northern laws.

When Wes had killed a dozen men
And soldiers chased him down,
He had to hide among his kin
And neighbors far from town.

So when three Yankee soldiers showed
And cornered him at last,
They didn't understand his code
From years already passed.

He turned and charged all three by horse
Which caught them by surprise,
Dispatching two with deadly force
Mid startled shouts and cries.

Wes told the last what he required:
"Submit to the South, or die!"
The soldier answered him with fire.
Wes shot him through the eye.

The local folks gave Wes their aid
For his courage gave them hope.
They buried the Yanks in a nearby glade
On a sandy hidden slope.

The law soon called him renegade,
But in his heart he knew
He rode for justice and repaid
The measure that was due.

TROUBLE-BOUND LOOSE

in and out of cuffs
but one day bound
for trouble, they caught
Wes on the road, lashed
his legs under a horse
with just a blanket
to pad the ride to jail

but didn't find
that extra tucked gun
in the pit of his arm

so when evening came
the first two busied
with camp and fire
and only one watched
while Wes walked
the stretch back
into his legs

that's when he made
as if to cry
doubled up and crossed
hands under arms
to come up shooting
onetwothree like that

so no one left
to ride away but him
and trouble-bound loose again

TERZA RIMA SNARE

His luck at cards was good that night
as was his generosity
beneath the gambling candlelight.

But his earnings prompted jealousy
and led a couple to devise
a trap that Wes just didn't see.

The woman caught him with her eyes
and promised love, though nothing pure,
through artful charms and easy lies.

He followed her and her allure
past closing bars and tabled chairs
with love the bait and her the lure.

She led him out and up the stairs
secluded to a private room
entangled with her wily snares.

She worked her spell through soft-lit gloom
when a man burst in to bluster threats
of honor's loss and Wes's doom.

The man then claimed a rightful debt
that only Wes's money paid
or else he'd call for quick arrest.

Wes recognized the trap they'd made
and offered pay for what was due
so their suspicions were allayed.

He fumbled, dropped a coin or two,
but when the thoughtless man kneeled down
he rose to find the ruse was through.

He grimaced in a sudden frown
to see a gun pressed to his head,
to hear the hammer's cocking sound.

He never felt the slug of lead
as Wes discharged the pistol ball
that slapped him back across the bed.

Reposed now on a bedsheet pall,
he learned too late, both late and dead,
to know your betters in a brawl.

DEATH BY SNORING

He shifted back his weight a bit
To ease the forward trotting pace.
His seat bones felt the saddle's fit
From running hard in a sudden haste.

He'd once again escaped the law
On a stolen horse that sealed his fate,
This gunman with a Texas drawl
Who killed too quick and thought too late.

That morning he had heard the sound
Come sawing through the floor and wall
Of a man who snored one story down
With a noise that echoed through the hall.

Too much to bear for one whose face
Betrayed a night of revelry,
He rose to give the man a taste
Of pistol-whipped civility.

But by the time he struck the door,
Had knocked it open for a fight,
The man was reaching toward the floor
To grab his gun in startled fright.

Wes shot him dead with one clean shot,
No chance for explanations now,
His reputation made his lot:
A fugitive who headed south.

ARMSTRONG

i

He crossed the boundary line without a thought,
a single horse's stride, and nothing changed
the Ranger's hard resolve, beyond his home
and Texas law—it made no difference—
no difference, for sure, to those who rode
beside him, captaining this band of men
intent to catch or kill, a thousand miles
away, the hardened gang of Swain's.
                                                    At best
it was Armstrong who wanted most of all
to see the code of justice done, for now
just easier to let the others ride
for bounty's sake, and leave his grief all tucked,
a saddlebag of saddened thoughts, best left
in lashed-up straps until the moment came.

ii

The riders made their way across the plains,
a trip they made by horse, and then by rail
and then by mount again. Their journey's steps
in grass began to give to bunched-up trees
and later forests, uneasy at times
to men accustomed to a line of fire
that fell before their line of sight.
                                                    Each night
The men would talk of home, of Texas hopes
or dreams of a more settled land, a place
where lawlessness would find no home.

Each night, Armstrong pulled the watch from the bag,
unwrapped it from the cloth and wound its stem,
perhaps, he thought, a way to keep a deed
alive in the mainspring, and mechanized
despite the lapses of his memory
or the soft pockets of dreams, from a time
not touched by grief.

      "John, you oughta give
that watch a rest," said Josh, who might have been
the youngest of the posse's group. "Besides,
don't do no good if all you do is stash
it back inside your bag. I never seen
you oncst a using it."

      "Don't pester John,"
Bill Dodd, it was, who spoke behind John's back.
"It don't concern you none."

      "Let the boy be,"
Armstrong said, and then to Josh, "This watch
belonged to Charlie Webb."

       The name had said
enough, for everyone in Texas knew
the tale.

    "So how'd you come by that?" Josh asked,
a kind of reverence began to swell
his eyes to match a four-bit piece.

"Don't you know nothing?" It was Dodd who spoke
again. "Armstrong here was his closest friend."

80

"And this here watch was his?"

"The widow Webb
give it to him." Dodd replied as though John
were mute.

Young Josh just couldn't let it be.
"I've heard tell Hardin shot him in the back."

"Then you heard wrong," John said begrudgingly.
It felt uncomfortable to give the likes
of Hardin any due. "But just the same
they gunned him down."

Then John just couldn't bring
himself to say the rest, how Webb had walked
by accident into his fate, had walked on by
and only then had recognized the face,
had turned to draw his gun, to stand behind
his sheriff's badge.

"Hardin, you're under arrest!"
In frozen stride, the desperado dropped
and twisted to the ground to turn and shoot
with cat-like moves. As Charlie tasted his words
the bullet ripped his cheek, and others fired
as well, Charlie unaware he'd faced off
all the gang and not just one, when he fell,
slug-riddled, and lifeless to the ground.

The truth be told, John's lawman code meant more
than capturing a single man or men.
He wanted justice, not revenge, and Webb's

own watch had come to represent a time
of new beginning ways, meant the time run out
for those who could not understand the change
of ways, more settled-down, across the land.

John packed the watch away, in afterthought
and to himself as much as to the boy,
he said, "Hardin's turn will come, it'll come
when we catch Swain, we'll catch the two at once."

iii

They rendezvoused with Pinkertons next day,
an intercepted note—a bit of luck
explained the whereabouts of Swain, his plans
to leave his newfound Pensacola home
to head back West, to hide among his clan.
both Pinkertons and Rangers had agreed
the gang was dangerous, they'd need surprise
to do it right.
                  The law in Florida
had sent a man named Hutch, who'd brought the news
they'd need: that Swain was headed home by train.

"We'll let him board, we'll let him settle in,
    get comfortable," said John. "Then jump him quick."

"While he's a napping," chimed in Dodd, and smiled
    a smile that reached the corners of his jaws.

iv

The day arrived, with all in readiness.
The Pinkertons then telegraphed: The man
had made the train, his hat and dress described
(to grab him quick), but he was not alone.
At least accompanied by one, or more,
who'd gotten on as well—unwelcome news,
not knowing just how many guns they'd find.

"We know Brown Bowen will be one," said Dodd,
whose fingers counted who they'd likely see.

"Who's he?" Josh asked.
                              "His sister is the one
that married Hardin. Brown and Hardin ride
the one beside the other, count on that."
Dodd's doubled fingers turned to three.
"And then there's Swain."
                              "That's gang enough to count,"
said John, and restless as the train approached.

A deputy, with Hutch, stepped on the train
up front, while John and Dodd and Josh jumped on
at last, and scrambled from their hiding place
for fear the gang might recognize, at least,
the Captain's face.
                              They waited in the rear
for Hutch to walk the aisle, reporting where
the desperados sat.

"It looks to be,"
said Hutch, when he sauntered up at last to John,
"that Swain has settled in the smoking car,
and next to him, a younger, plucky gun."

"Just two?" Dodd's doubled fingers stirred the air.
"You didn't see a sign of Bowen—Brown
I mean—or any sign of Hardin's face?
That's not enough. If Hardin's there and sees
us first . . . This ain't a bit to my liking, John."

"You four go in and make to rush them two,"
said John. "I'll cover you behind in case
there's more."
                They all could see John's jaw was set,
and so the plan was made, since John it was
alone who'd know the others' looks. With stealth
they eased inside the car, the rearward door
ajar, while Armstrong peeked inside to watch
the others make their way toward plumes of smoke
as Swain sucked at a meerschaum pipe, seated
the closest to the aisle.
                        From Armstrong's view,
he saw them work their way, to get up close
then saw them rush the seated man at last.
Swain struggled hard, but finally couldn't fight
with the black-jack fall of a pistol's smack,
the barrel like a boom and lowered quick
so it left Swain all heaped, unconsciously,
and tumble-splayed across the floor.
                                John's eyes

gripped the motion of the younger man, saw
him start to draw his gun, which prompted John
to fire across the mayhem in the car,
to shoot to kill, the struggle's final act,
and brought the fracas to a halt.

"We better look for Hardin," Dodd called out.

"No need. You've got him pinned there on the floor."
Armstrong's finger pointed down at Swain.
"I knew he'd changed his name, he couldn't change
his face. I didn't want to take the chance
you'd shoot him down. I promised Charlie's wife
I'd try to bring him back alive."
                              "And what
of Brown?"
                    "Guess he didn't make the train,
but then, that only made it easier,
and you can bet, we only have to bide
our time."
              John drew and let a heavy sigh
escape his chest, then shackled Hardin's hands.
A part of him could finally rest, the part
that now could let old Charlie's watch be still,
could let the pent-up force that drove the hands
relax, no longer now a part of time,
and time to let the tensioned spring of grief
wind down, the ticking to an end at last.

SONNET FOR JANE

He loved her for the way she looked at dawn,
The way she always tended family,
The way she always loved him faithfully
Despite the many times that he was gone.
He loved her for her steady gaze, so strong
Yet so forgiving, and the quality
That made his wife, his Jane, so womanly
And right when other people called him wrong.

They had so little time of quiet peace,
So little time to share in love and trust,
So little time when he was there, at least,
And tried to overcome his wanderlust.
The best part of his life had also ceased
The day she died, her loneliness released.

A LIFE OF STRIFE

Wes always found a path that led to strife.
Rebellious as he was, confined to jail,
he never could accept the rules of life.

He plotted his escape and so contrived
to tunnel underground and out, his tale
was bound to find a path that led to strife

and jealous tongues. Betrayed and undermined,
the plot, uncovered now and doomed to fail,
confirmed his take on rules of life.

The floggings only gave him tougher hide,
confined for weeks that made his skin grow pale,
so typical of him to cling to strife.

Yet Wes was smart enough at last to bide
his time, to try to correspond by mail
with those who understood those rules, and life.

But by the time that he was free, his wife
was gone and all his plans, it seemed, derailed.
So still he found a path that led to strife
and once again denounced all rules for life.

TWO-SIDED COIN

never made much sense
the lawmen he could buy
with nothing but a smile

easy to see that boy-face
planted young on shoulders
and so easy to forget

the quick of his hands
and even quicker temper
with a killing finger-squeeze

the law and lawless
two sides
of a flipped coin

one side just
like the understanding other
and maybe the sense of why

so many signed their names
to see him free with time
unreckoned and due

INSIDE-OUTSIDE

The card-play lasted	The card-play lasted
long into night,	long past light,
his mind hard-tamped	the room too cramped
with drink and smoke.	for coat or cloak,
But with each lost	as coins were tossed
hand, the lamp glowed	to winning hands and flowed
indifferently, new-fangled	indifferently, untangled
and lit with current,	from tight fingers and sent
no taper to trim	to strike the table's rim,
away the passing time,	or stacked up in a line.
no flicker-fire	When all began to tire
to judge the new	and thought the game was through
against the old,	with all sums said or told
or the trickled loss	and folded hands a toss
of what he'd been.	away, Hardin, drunk again,
He drew his gun	had drawn his pointed gun
and pointed at the lamp	at the dealer, damp
beyond the dealer's ear.	now with sweat and fear.
"This just ain't right.	"This just ain't right.
I want it back."	I want it back."
He hardly saw	The dealer had to draw
the money lost in sport	the money out and short
pushed his way.	those luckier at play.

"I only want what's lost."   "I only want what's lost."

But finding only coins,   Made nervous by these goings-
which he scooped up,   on, the others anteed up
he staggered out   then watched him stagger out
the door and into dark.   the door and into dark.

so boys, you know me well. you know as well
i've lived on both sides of the law, and now
it's time to throw myself on mercy's door.
i can't deny, i killed john wesley hardin.
you also know, like me, that now the world
is better off, and i cain't rightly say
.i'd do it differently. it's not like i
was unprovoked.
        and yes it's maybe true
i shot him in the back, but that was still
in self-defense.
        you know my oldest boy,
if only he had steered all clear, and walked
the other way when hardin's woman, drunk
and loud, had waved that pistol in the street.
if only he had just forgot that he
was deputy. it's not like we don't have
enough El Paso law. no, he had to walk
right up and pull that gun of hers away.
he had to take her in, and when her man
showed up, all riled and hot and dandered up,
she'd said how she was sorry, and that
was what had got his goat, to say as much
to any law.
        and hardin now a man
of law, a lawyer, now ain't that a spit
in justice's face? i know, i know, he served
his time, but that don't change him none at all.
i heard he kept her on her knees all night,

his gun a pointed at her head to make
her say her sorries, not to him so much
as to the lord, for breaking down in front
of any other man but him. what kind
of man would treat another human soul
like that, i ask? did he deserve to live?

but i coulda let it pass, if only
he had let things go, if only that black
heart of his had not commenced to taunt
my son, had not commenced to threaten life.
like righteousness belonged to him alone,
like none of his or him could do no wrong.

so when i saw him in the street and saw
his glare, i walked right up and told him just
as much as i am telling you. it's then
and there he said it.
                    selman i'll go get a gun
and meet you soon enough and when i come
i'll come on smokin. then i'll make you shit
just like a dog and all around the block.

well, boys, the sun was plenty hot that day
and sweat was falling from my face alright,
and maybe, yeah, i felt a bit of dog
begin to work my bowels, but we all know
how he could be when once he got a thing
all worked around inside that head of his.

i still believe he paid them guns, the ones
last spring that killed mcrose, him sitting there
at home and holding beulah's hand and her
not drunk, not yet, for all the time they'd lived
in sin. not knowing yet that hardin had
her husband killed. no wonder that he wore
that metal plate beneath his vest, but still
I swear there weren't no need, a man whose heart
was hard as that.
                          and everyone of you
could say as well as me that all those folks
that followed him around, and just to get
a look, saw signs of what he once had been,
or maybe some had turkey vulture eyes
and saw the look of death come closing in.
or sure he had that hard-drink face that comes
from years of living wild, that wasted him
away 'til nothing much was left but mean.

so when he said he'd get a gun, I knew
my only chance would be to try to get
the drop on him, to even up the odds.

so all that day, while he was in his cups,
i kept up watch but always out of sight.
he drank away the afternoon and played
at cards and dice. the evening turned to dark
and best as i can recollect, the time
was drawing nigh to midnight when i poked
my head inside the room and saw him there.
his back was to the door, all comfortable
with elbows propped up on the bar and still
at dice.
                i paced the boards along the length
of san antonio, the street by now
deserted so i kept a silent watch,
the wide door of the acme saloon ajar.
i knew i'd waited long enough and then
i saw my chance: a man pushed through the door
to leave and in i slipped, my gun in hand.

i watched him slide a worn-out box of dice
before the man who stood beside his right.
i heard him,
                    that's my sixes four to beat.

by then i wasn't more than a pace away
and shouted out,

        who's smoking now?

he might have flipped his coat tails out, he might
have started then to turn. i didn't wait
but shoved my .45 up close behind
and fired into his head. i fired again
and then again.

        don't shoot him anymore,
he's dead, i heard a voice behind me say.

i looked down on the deed i'd done at last.
the fingers held his pistol grip, the gun
half drawn and pulled, but a half-drawn gun
in hardin's hand meant death for one of us,
and how can anyone of you blame me
for choosing him instead?

        i tell you, what
i did was right. i killed to stay alive.

EPILOGUE

My mother's mother's voice was silent then,
her eyelids wrinkled with the years, and closed,
dreaming deep into a world I'd never know.
She'd made no lesson of her family's tale
and maybe just some history to please
of what she knew of cousins now long dead.

But still I couldn't help, I had to ask
about the time she'd said I had his look.
Her eyes still closed, she answered quietly,
"His look? I guess you do — you've got his blood,
just never let it make you turn away."
From home, I knew she meant.
                              Though now I live
a thousand miles away, and seldom make
the visit back. I never seem to find
the time these days, and even if I think
I'll call, I don't.
                    I guess it's in the blood,
this westering, this restlessness, this song.

tamped, but loose

enough to breathe

TAMPED, BUT LOOSE
ENOUGH TO BREATHE

It's not that bitch, necessity—
whose musings purport
to guide invention's guile—
but fear herself, unsung

goddess of primal paste,
who twists gristle
to hang meat on nightmares.
Don't underestimate *that* gal.

Take Poe, who plucked
strings to quicken Angst
of burial alive, so vigorous,
pages of Sears & Roebuck once

sold toe-attaching cord
to jangle graveyard bells
atop a town of mounds,
where even sextants assured

they'd tamp earth loose
enough for jiggle room.
How's that for a siren taunt
from that little girl?

In fact, it's still
her voice that tamps
quotidian, seething life
just loose enough to breathe.

FEARFUL SYMMETRY

"Oh no! Who let that stegosaur back in?"
(It's all I hear above their din, their cries.)
"His formal bulk offends us once again."

I lumber up the steps without a friend
in sight, but hardly find it much surprise
they'd ask, "Who let that stegosaur back in?"

I waddle down the halls with no amends.
My fearful symmetry cannot disguise
how much my form offends them yet again.

I chortle with Jurassic joy to bend
their simple imagist and shapeless lies
by swinging wide my stegosaur back end

to hammer at the walls, to maim and rend
with cadenced lines. With glee I swing my spikes
to bludgeon their effete offense again.

Their asteroidal lips cannot defend
their boring songs. I dismiss those voices that despise
the way they've let a stegosaur back in
to frolic in a formal world again.

ZEST IN AN ISLE BEGUILED

"That's Grandmother's home, the Isle of Föhr,"
she said, and pointed, map-beguiled
by the flattened name, no trace of frigid
North Sea blustering sandblast wind
on the longitude of dreams, my wife
determined to touch her mothering roots.

Her Nordic blue eyes and blonded roots
as strong a compass tug to Föhr
as magnet north, tugged my wife
and me, along, at last beguiled
as well. Assured romantic winds
could blow away all thought of frigid

landscapes through postcards tacked to fridge, it
never occurred to us its wind-
mills needed wind, or trees their roots
to stand against the gales on Föhr,
Circe's song so strong it beguiled
our undeterred delight. So when my wife

and I arrived, aghast, my wife
unsteady in the steady frigid
winter blast (but so beguiled
were we to believe that even roots
in a dampened January Föhr
could soften into breeze such wind.)

We. Were. Wrong. The breeze was wind
and the place as cold as hell to wife
and daughter (come along) to Föhr,
the mothering land, and so frigid
fucking cold that a week with their roots
collapsed to overnight, beguiled

or not. Enchanting isle, beguiled
and beguiling—or not. Veneered with wind,
a place where dreams could GO TO…well, root,
to grow for mothers, daughters, and wives
from scenes on picture cards less frigid
than footing the coasts on Föhr.

Yet, less beguiled, it's still my wife
whose dreams unremember frigid winds,
still touch roots, enchanting her, and Föhr.

MAJOR ARCANA 0

Lad and dog (foolish pair),
fooled to think, fooled, impaired,
unfettered, go striding
foot to foot, everywhere

unharried, colliding
with strangers politely
stepping wide, yielding room,
this pair intertwining

strident strides, whistled tunes.
Each will know all too soon
their path will abruptly
summon fate—signal doom.

Not snobbish nor stuffy,
not fickle nor huffy,
blind to paths' steep descents,
a tortured compunction.

Lad and dog without sense,
doomed to fall *sans* pretense,
free to fall, falling free,
lad and dog, suddenly.

GHOST WRITERS

We've decided now's the time to rewrite
our bios. Perhaps a science fiction
or some ramped-up version of our life

— for future fans, who'd opt for sights
of wide-screen worlds in contravention.
We'll star, of course, when it's time to write

the scene where all the Earth's at height-
ened high alert, or at collision's
door, ramping up our scripted life

with light sabers flashing for viewers' delight.
Weakened and scorched, in true affliction,
we persevere in time to right

what's wrong—well, maybe not that trite!
But still, two bios worth inscription:
finaléd, bold and amped up lives

where order's restored when we exit (stage right).
Just a bit of flourish to our rendition
now that we think we might rewrite
more ramped-up versions of our life.

THE STRAW MAN

(with apologies to Wallace Stevens)

Maybe you need shit for brains
to regard how muck taints straw
in a stall dumpling'd with horse apples;

and must callous your eyes
to behold the mounds thicken with heaps,
the ground ripe in the gathering swell

of an August afternoon; and not to think
of any more in the sound of soft heaves,
in the sound of clump-tumbles,

which is the sound of decay
full of the same soft tumbles
that will cover what was bare straw

for the digger, who digs into horse apples,
and, shoveling alone, beholds
not shoveling to come but the shoveling soon gone.

TIMOROUS TRIGONOMETRIES

"The limit of 'the secant line' is 'the tangent line.'"
– John H. Matthews & Russell W. Howell,
"The Tangent Parabola" in The AMATYC Review

Their remarks cut seldom
perpendicular, nor to the heart's
core,
   hers a secant
of intent, an entry aimed
to exit near his fleshed
circle of defense, and bleeding

thin remorse.
     But truer
than his glancing tangents,
never deep enough to bruise
or leave a scar worth
healing.
    These geometers
who dally, who trig
with shallow words
that never touch.

PITCH

Well, we had him for a full two years
while his body grew to fit those ears.

He had teeth enough inside his mouth
but he didn't know the north from the south.

So we led him up to meet our mare.
First, all he did was gawk and stare.

Why he champed his lips like a baby horse
until finally! Nature changed his course.

Yeah, all of a sudden he measured up
and proved that he was horse enough.

He stepped to the plate, gave it a shot.
(We'll know in three weeks if she's bred—or not!)

Now he struts around. Oh, he's cock of the walk
Though he's mostly brag, mostly talk.

The piper's tune is a year away
to pay his keep as a stud all day.

And if he don't, then that's okay.
There's more like him just burning hay.

The pasture's still got lots of room
—and a swipe of the knife can change his tune.

FAITHLESS

it's almost like sex
in some ways better
the pencil's glide
toward the final letter
a poem that fits
that moves that breathes
with rhythmical strokes
that are meant to please

it comes on a whim
it comes as surprise
it's good when it's true
but works when it lies
its words caress,
and tease, build
with frenzied lust
'til the paper's filled

and when it's through
the joy all done
I look for a poem
with words still unsung
it's not that I love
the old one less
but an untried poem
seduces best

AFTER THE BEEP

1

The last I knew
we were copasetic, but that's
the last I knew.
I didn't know that you were through
with us and all our scrapes and scraps.
We'd weathered all our former spats
the last I knew.

2

I called to say
I miss you so—that's all. That's what
I called to say.
Give me a ring, just to allay
my fears and anxious heart, it's not
a lot to ask, it's just a thought,
I called to say.

3

For what it's worth
I'm over you—I know we're through,
for what it's worth.
I'm sorry if my tone is terse.
Down deep I thought our love was true
and wish you shared the same thought, too,
for what it's worth.

4

Go screw yourself!
I just found out you'd slept around,
so screw yourself,
and may you burn in deepest hell!
Who needs the grief, that's what I've found,
you bitchy, slimy, two-faced clown,
go screw yourself!

5

Oh. My mistake.
I just found out it wasn't you.
That's my mistake.
My friends' poor joke in such poor taste.
Of course, I knew it wasn't true,
so maybe we could start anew
from my mistake.

6

Okay, okay,
I know what's done is done and past,
okay, okay.
I called to say I'll go away
for what it's worth. You're free at last.
Our love is sliced, it's diced and hashed,
okay—okay?

7

You there? Hello?
I've been thinking ... it's not too late.
You there? Hello?
We've both cooled off a bit and so
for what it's worth I called to say
it's my mistake to hesitate.
You there? Hello?

COLLIMATION

Star light, star bright,
first star I see tonight
I wish I may, I'd like to hope
to see more through this telescope.

I bought it just a month ago,
arriving at the moon's full glow
so strong I couldn't see a star,
too shy to twinkle from afar.

It took a week to douse the moon
and give a proper darkling gloom.
All set, I was, to then begin
since where I live is dark as sin.

It's far from artificial light,
just made for telescopic sight.
I laugh at townies' light pollution.
From where I stand a solved solution.

I point the scope to slew into
the night's celestial distant views,
but everything is blurred at first—
my observations still are cursed.

No star reveals itself to me.
The sky is still a sight unseen.
I check the scope from top on down
with scowling face and somber frown.

At last I read the explanation:
it seems the scope needs collimation.
The mirror must be set, just so
to give the line of sight some flow.

I tinker with my best finesse,
but soon it sees not more, but less.
I vow to persevere, I will
defeat the mocking stars with skill.

The month goes by, but undeterred
I tinker though my dander's stirred.
Again, the moon begins to show
with me still just as blind below.

Star light, star bright,
first star I see tonight
I wish I may, I'd like to hope
to see more through this telescope.

But then again, the sky's so vast
I'll never see the first or last.
Best thought of as oracular—
best seen through small binoculars!

severed dreams

HUNTER'S SONG

It takes a night-adjusted eye
to stalk the dark,
and the hand must have a hunter's gait,
a stealth that doesn't overrun
the distant smudge of galaxies.

You must pursue their ghost and glow,
easing up, gently, as they drink
from nearby pools of light, or lap
at the milked edges of the void.

Now, hold your breath, don't look
directly at the thing, too shy to take
the bold stare of your eye.
Steal a glance and let its shape
accustom to your sight.

Only a hunter's gaze can find
the look-back time, stretched
by years of light and space,
etched with the line from sight to seen.

And then, only then, taste
the hunt, the capture
of your prey in gathered light.
Let your throat fill with silence,
with a mouth full of awe.

PAPER TRAIL
The Papyrus Museum, Berlin

The canons of the dead
scroll into endless reams,
though quieted, unread
as tomes, intoned between

the scrolls and endless reams
a message often found
in tomes, but the tone beneath
dismissed, like a prince uncrowned

or a theme refused, unfound
by a rash and present sweep
too occupied to crown
or homage such scripts, their heap

discarded with a sweep.
The present is all we are,
scant homage for these heaps
of brittled thoughts afar,

these canons of the dead,
unquiet, seldom read.

COLD WAR LIES

"We choose ... to do the other things, not because
they are easy, but because they are hard."
                        —JFK's moon speech, 1962

He snaps off the transistor
voice, choosing the hard things,
more concerned with politics in hand:
the rigged feel of a borrowed
boat, the smile on a borrowed wife—

both sheen with the sun's stamp
as the bow halves water, like open
legs furrowing foam at the stern.
He tugs sheets that strain, that scarf
sky when the sloop tacks

to face tasted brine, allowing breeze
to lift her skirt, too revealing
intentioned thought, their isolation
clandestine under a spanned blue,
choosing the reach of a far shoal

to anchor in spent waves—and not
because it is easy, but because
it's wrong—while seaweeds bump
the hull with faceless scalps: all lies
in innuendo, some lies unsaid.

RUMBLE STRIPS

i.

I've hit that strumming strip
again, must veer my car,
strumming asphalt chatter,
to over steer straying

ways, my fault to lapse
into errant vectors.
Perhaps it's my absent eye
that alights to attach thought

to thought as it grasps broken
shards of light, splintering
prisms in glass—bright scars
adorning tar or ditch.

I need to stitch my mind
To straits near the center line.

ii.

Why can't life have rumble
strips? I'm not asking for God
to stutter staccato clarion
klaxon chirps, but simply
soft *ex machina* burps
on my behest, to halt
my wanders to left, or right.
Should some toad, unbidden, spry,

vault from my mouth, how about
a trumpeting throat to drown
my blather? What I need
is rumbling—replies on High
with clatter—to trounce my penchants
for impudent, hasty indignance.

MOUNTAIN ROADS

The roads I still like best
struggle to bridge two points
strung out rubbery thin,
like a hat ear to ear
with its band tearing free
from a warped fitting brim.

The good roads rattle time
with washboard, rock-hard ruts,
tire-chewing the day's pace
to no more than a walk,
stretching distance the same
as any stretch of miles.

A proper road resists
travel for the end's sake,
like unwalked hiking trails
that vanish at our feet,
making us search the land's lay
as we stride ground with care.

It's watchful journeyed roads
that can draw in our thoughts,
naked, honestly fixed
on what each bend brings, each
lurch in the grade ahead.
Roads worth the traveling.

REPOPULATING PARADISE

Contrails bale the land's bucket,
connecting Earth to East,
dangling below, hardly Edenic,
unshambled by shear-face

emblazoned sky-gauzed wires
to our earnest West
in duns sifting sun's gold,
shouldering rock,

archeological ossuaries,
unrivaled rivers,
the cry of the unchristened
by tarnished talismans

opting for unguent
overreaching the plaint
crests soon heard
in the turgid flow,

filtered, flushed,
broom grass beds
or a misted remorse,
of deserts, destined,

free to seek
in unbidden plains,
mulled hearts
reduced to sand,

garnished with grit,
opened wide to winds
in a wanton West,
calamitous, lurid

gore, gullets
wailing solitude
or weaning kin
with lessoned life.

WOUNDED KNEE
(June, 1992)

A trickle scratches creek
sand, shallowing the valley.
Our Oglala guide, an Elder,
wears ravines deep-faced
as time, old as tears,

when he points at a far-bank
ridge, a finger tracing dry air
on vanished cavalry's crossfire.
Wind soughs at the far slope,
could almost be the screams

of his grandfathers rising
from trenched graves,
where grass struggles
to cover memories (some say)
of children, women, old men.

Red tobacco ties tatter
a single monument, crowded
by fences, while ghosts
battle breezes, no more
than a shudder on cottonwoods.

APOSTROPHE APOLOGY

It's your own fault, you know,
if your babble makes me steal
your liquid breath, parting earthy
lips, banked and sloped to coax
watery moans from your rising
murmur. Relax, it's just
an irrigated intubation to guide
your sigh onto ground clenched
too long by six-foot deep silences
of frost.
       And now to hear you vibrate
audible songs over smooth rocks,
log jammed, and more than I can
stand when your whisper swells.
So I trache you with steel-
ribbed straws until grass chatters
with the sibilant substance
of your flow. I promise
not to steal too much, too long.
But please, please sing on.

THE LIVES OF DOGS

Why do the lives of dogs
seem hardly to matter?
Is it our calloused care
that shapes their narrow lot,
that heaps them, happenstance,
with what we want from them?
For they can best express
the most that ever we
could be or say aloud —
at least more honestly.

Or then again, perhaps
they can say no such thing,
living in worlds apart
and never meant for us,
yet sharing what they can
from generosity,
a pretence that our plight
could somehow matter,
peopling dog worlds by chance —
an embarrassed mistake.

A RECIPE FOR PIE
—For the Celebration of Ann Gery's Life

First of all, let's make it
clear, this pie is not common
pie, it's made to end all pies,
and when it's done, aroma
good as taste will linger on
for years, and even years.

As for ingredients, just make do,
make it with what comes your way,
make it full of flavors from home
and life, and you can always find
the sweetness of a friend
to cancel out a bitter word.

Make sure the crust is made from scratch.
It's got to last 'til the pie is gone.
And it's easier to knead the husband in
from the start, but not too smooth, a gob
of husband will have lumps, they come
that way, and then add fire with care.
Crust needs heat—not scorched
or brittle but so the edges hold
for all the filling to come.

Now the fun part: Add love and just
a dash of zest for life, then briskly stir
until the children come. A pinch of heartache
brings out flavor, but sprinkle in
a palmful of work and season well
with zeal and all the hope and joy
that you can stand, and next
blend it with those secret things
that suit your tongue—an acumen
for politics adds spice, and movies
help it all to rise and match
imagination's flights and fitted fancies.

The cooking's done before you know
and there for all to eat,
there for all the lip-smacking
teeth-and-tongue torrents of taste.

And later, when the kitchen light
is out, the home quiet,
the cook gone, aroma still remains,
and memories fresh with wildberry sweets,
a lingering across the house
that tells you when the pie is done.

A pie worth the making, after all.

WHY I READ BOOKS
(for my mother, on her 80ᵗʰ birthday)

It's probably my mother's fault,
those many childhood years ago.
My brother and I tucked in bed,
our toes squirming to form pockets
under the stretched sheath of our sheets.

Our eyelids curtained into sleep
as the spell-cast of her voice
lifted deeds from flat pages,
flinging them through twilight doors
or windowed young imaginings —

Hero-descending journeys traced
tangled thread to Minotaur tales,
to rivers, darkly filled with "styx,"
to caves with three-headed snapping dogs,
or homes hoveled by blind hags.

"You are what you read," my mother said.
She wanted adventure to fill
our dreams—and, in fact, there were nights,
balanced on night's thin cusp,
when I was never really sure

but what my own small hand
guided a sword's level sweep —
there, at my feet, writhing tendrils
circled Medusa's frozen stare,
her severed dreams replaced by my own.

MARK TODD is the recipient of the 2017 Karen Chamberlain Lifetime Achievement Award for Colorado Poetry, and he has appeared on both Colorado Public Radio and the Travel Channel representing his work. He founded Western's Graduate Program in Creative Writing, where he has been Professor of English at Western since 1988, and serves as Contributing Editor for Western Press Books. He has 30 years of professional journalism experience, having published hundreds of news stories, features, columns, and editorials in local through international markets. He also served as editor and publisher of both a newspaper and a regional magazine and, at one point, digested online news for the Lycos daily news service. Mark has performed his poetry across the country and in Europe. His books include two collections of poetry, a science fiction novel, and as co-author with wife Kym O'Connell-Todd a comedy/fantasy trilogy and a creative nonfiction book about hauntings in frontier mining towns of the Rocky Mountains. Three of his books were nominated for Colorado Book Awards and one was also nominated for the Colorado Blue Spruce Award.

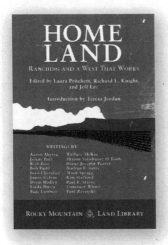
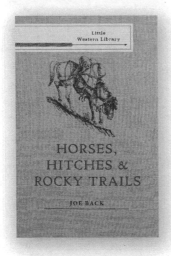

BOWER HOUSE

Passionate about the environment, telling
great stories, and living the good life through
fantastic food, inspiring literature, broad
travel, and the outdoors.

Wire Song: Poems
Mark Todd

ISBN 978-0-9657159-9-7
US $13.95

Heading Home: Field Notes
Peter Anderson

ISBN 978-1-942280-21-7
US $14.99